Islamic Belief and Practice

Jan Thompson

Hodder & Stoughton

LONDON SYDNEY AUCKLAND TORONTO

Copyright © 1981 Jan Thompson

First published in Great Britain 1981
Seventh impression 1990

British Library Cataloguing in Publication Data

Thompson, Jan
  Islamic belief and practice.
  1. Islam
  2. Title
  297   BP45

  ISBN 0-7131-0586-0

Printed in Great Britain for Edward Arnold, the
educational, academic and medical publishing division of
Hodder and Stoughton Limited, Mill Road, Dunton Green,
Sevenoaks, Kent by St Edmundsbury Press Limited,
Bury St Edmunds, Suffolk.

Preface

There should no longer be any need to convince schools of the merits of teaching world religions if our pupils are to understand the world of today. It is a world which seems to be getting ever smaller as communications via television and travel bring us into contact with foreign parts. Indeed we rub shoulders with people of different beliefs and customs in our everyday lives. The Muslim world in particular is frequently being brought to our attention. Since the news media are mainly interested in the economic, the spectacular or the macabre, we hear most about soaring oil prices, the wealth of Arab visitors to this country and the severity of traditional punishments. It is up to the schools to help their pupils to put things in their right perspective. Toleration of other people will only come from a balanced understanding of what they stand for. An ability to evaluate other people's ideas and to discriminate between them must be based on a true understanding of them.

This book explains the beliefs and practices of Islam for pupils in the middle years of secondary school. It tries to express what Muslims themselves mean by these beliefs and practices and why they follow them. It does not concentrate on Muslim history and culture since there are already many worthy books which do that. It brings in only so much history as is necessary to understand the implications of the Islamic faith today; and it has been found necessary to go back constantly to Muhammad, whose life forms the framework for the whole book. This also helps us to see the ideals of Islam, to which Muslims aspire.

As for Religious Education, it is true that the various dimensions of religion can be taught from any world religion, be it Hinduism, Christianity, Islam or any other. In a society shaped by Christianity, however, this must surely be the first concern and then one needs to see to what extent other religions are represented among the members of the school. Yet at least some other religions must be looked at if only to put across the diversity of the religious phenomenon. Islam must surely rank high in the choice, for it is a monotheistic religion with much in common with Christianity and therefore is not such a big step for the pupils to take in terms of understanding the concepts involved.

Contents

With love to my daughter, Rebecca.
'Peace be on you and God's blessings.'

1 Islam

The religion of Islam, as we know it, began 1,350 years ago in Arabia (see Fig.1) with the man Muhammad. Some people mistakenly call this religion Muhammadanism. This is wrong because Muhammad is not worshipped; only God is worshipped in Islam. In fact, Muslims claim that their religion originated long before Muhammad, with Abraham, the first known worshipper of the one God.

The correct name for the religion is 'Islam'. This means 'surrender' and Muslims are those who surrender themselves to God (see Fig. 3(5) on page 9). All of us, at some stage in our lives, surrender ourselves to someone else's wishes or commands. Children are expected to do as they are told by their parents and teachers; and even adults have to obey the laws of society. Muslims believe that God is the highest authority of all and that his will must be obeyed at every stage of life. 'Islam' is also connected with the word for 'peace' and Muslims believe that obeying God is the only way for men and women to find real satisfaction, happiness and peace with themselves.

Islam has many followers and is the second largest religion in the world, after Christianity. It is difficult to be quite sure of the figure for we do not know exactly how many live in the Communist lands of China and the Soviet Union, and estimates vary widely: between 500 million and double that number (see Fig.15 on page 59). Like all large religions, Islam has developed in different ways as it has grown and there are now various parties within it. There are two main schools of thought: Sunni and Shi'a. The majority are Sunnis, who account for about 85 per cent of all Muslims. Their name means that they consider themselves to be following the right 'path' of Islam. The other fifteen per cent are the Shi'ites. Within these two divisions are other minor groups.

Despite this variety, there is a feeling of unity and brotherhood amongst Muslims and there are several reasons for this. Although they live all over the world, they all look to Mecca in Arabia as their centre. Although they speak different languages in their everyday lives, they all learn their holy book, the Koran, in Arabic. Finally,

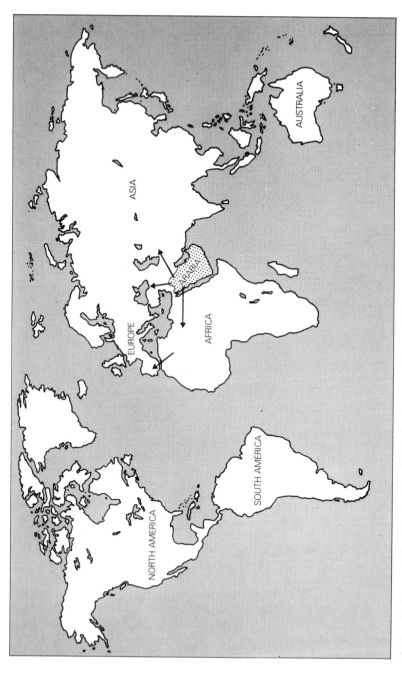

Fig.1. Muhammad lived in Arabia. By his death most of the Arabian peninsula was Islamic. Within the next century Islam spread across North Africa into Spain, and also into Palestine, Syria, Persia, and beyond into Central Asia.

2

all Muslims over the age of ten accept the same five duties. These are:

1 To believe in one God (Allah) and that Muhammad is his Prophet.
2 To pray five times a day.
3 To pay the Muslim tax which goes to charity.
4 To fast each year during the month of Ramadan.
5 To go on pilgrimage to Mecca at least once in their life if practicable.

These duties are often known as the *five pillars of Islam* since they are as essential to Islam as pillars are to the building they hold up. Every Muslim over the age of ten accepts them as binding upon himself. It is with these beliefs and practices that we shall be concerned mainly in this book.

Make sure you know
1 when Islam began
2 the names of the two main schools of thought in Islam
3 the five pillars of Islam

See if you understand
4 why this religion is called 'Islam'
5 how Muslims are united

Issues to discuss
6 How important do you think the basic unity of Islam is, both for its members, and in its efforts to convert outsiders?
7 Do you think it is important for a religion to lay down very clearly-defined beliefs and practices for its members, as Islam does in the five pillars?

3

2 Muhammad

The commonest phrase on a Muslim's lips is the Shahada, or formal declaration of faith. It is always spoken in Arabic and means:

There is no God but God
(and) Muhammad is the Prophet of God.

From this first pillar of Islam you can see the importance of Muhammad. He is not worshipped as divine but is honoured above all men as God's last and greatest prophet. A prophet is someone through whom God speaks to his people and Muslims recognise that there were other prophets before Muhammad: men like Abraham, Moses and Jesus. But they believe that these were sent to particular peoples whereas Muhammad was intended to bring God's words to all mankind. They say that the prophecies of those before him had been forgotten or altered, whereas the words spoken by God through Muhammad have been accurately recorded in the Koran for later generations so that there is no need for further prophecy. So Muslims believe that Muhammad was *the* Prophet, *the* Messenger of God, who did not start a new religion so much as bring people back to the right worship of the true God.

Muslims hold Muhammad in such respect that when they speak his name they add 'May the peace and blessings of God be upon him'. When they write down his name they often add the letters 's.a.s.' which stand for the above phrase, being the first letters of the Arabic words for it. Furthermore, they never allow Muhammad to be represented in any way. There are no pictures or statues of him since Muslims are not really allowed to portray the human form, nor would they permit a film on the life of Muhammad, with an actor taking his part.

Looking back on Muhammad and seeing how important he has been in the history of mankind, Muslims now view him with uncritical praise. They regard everything he did and said as perfect. One Muslim writer says this about him:

We must turn to Prophet Muhammad...if we want to see the picture of an ideally happy and pious married life and of a wise, just and benevolent ruler whom nothing could corrupt or divert

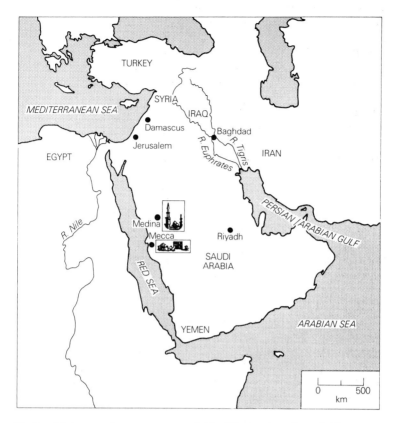

Fig.2. Muhammad spent most of his life in the city of Mecca, an important trading and religious centre for the Arabs. It became the centre of Islam. The last ten years of his life were lived in Medina where Muhammad established the first Islamic state. These are both in present day Saudi Arabia whose capital city is Riyadh.

from working for the material and moral amelioration of his people. Prophet Muhammad witnessed both the phases of persecution and success. He showed rare patience, fortitude, courage and love for his foes as a persecuted preacher of religion and in the hours of deepest gloom, and unparalleled self-control and mercy when his bitterest foes were helpless before him. (from *Islam and Christianity* by Mrs. Ulfat Aziz-us-Samad, distributed by the Islamic Cultural Centre)

As happens with all great men, legends grew up about Muhammad. One such legend tells of how Bahira, a Christian monk, gave Muhammad hospitality when he was travelling in the desert as a boy. Bahira had been sent a dream in which God told

5

him that a prophet would visit him with a mark between his shoulders. Bahira looked at Muhammad's back and there was the sign. How much history there is in such legends is debatable, particularly if they are of a person's childhood before he became well-known; but for the religious person they have a truth of their own. Legends such as these express what Muslims believe to be true about Muhammad: that God had chosen him from the very beginning of his life and even when Muhammad was still a little boy, God was shaping him for his future work.

The chief importance of Muhammad lay in the fact that he spoke God's words to the people and not his own words. Muhammad is thought to have acted as God's mouthpiece, merely reciting the words which were given to him. It is these words which form the Koran. Yet Muhammad's own words and actions were also taken note of and used by Muslims as an example by which to live. After his death, the traditions of what Muhammad said and did were collected and became known as the Hadith. The Koran itself often gives general guidelines rather than detailed rules as to how to live, and so Muslims have naturally turned to the life of Muhammad to see how the Koran can be put into practice. When quoting from the Koran, Muslims say 'God said . . .', but when quoting a Tradition they say 'The Prophet said . . .'. For example:

> The Prophet said: 'No one eats better food than that which he eats out of the work of his own hand. God did not raise a prophet but that he pastured goats. Yes! I used to pasture them for the people of Mecca.'

So we must remember when studying Islam that Muhammad's chief importance is as the Messenger of God who is believed to have brought the words of God directly to mankind—words which now make up the Koran. But he is also important as a man, for he demonstrated how to live a God-fearing life. He is a model for all Muslims to follow:

> The modern man, who has to lead a life as a son, a husband, a father, a poor worker, a citizen, a neighbour, a despised advocate of new ideas and ways, a victim of religious and political bigotry, a man with authority, a successful leader of man, a soldier, a business-man, a judge, and a ruler, will find Prophet Muhammad as a perfect model for him in all situations and walks of life. (from *Islam and Christianity*)

Therefore we shall be looking both at the Koran and at the man Muhammad as we try to understand more about Islam.

Make sure you know
1 the two main titles given to Muhammad
2 what is meant by a prophet
3 what the Hadith of Islam are about

See if you understand
4 why Muslims do not regard Islam as a new religion
5 why Muhammad is considered to be the last prophet

Issues to discuss
6 Why do you think legends have grown up about Muhammad's birth and childhood, as they have about most other great religious leaders?
7 Why is it that Muhammad is revered by Muslims? What types of heroes do people have today?

3 Prayer

The whole of a Muslim's life is affected by his religion. The first words spoken in the ears of a newborn baby are 'Allahu Akbar'— 'God is Most Great', and the same words are repeated at the burial of the dead. Throughout their lives Muslims are reminded of the greatness of God and of their dependence on him. This is shown particularly in the practice of the second pillar of Islam, that of prayer or salat.

Muslims must pray five times a day at the following times:

1 just before sunrise
2 between midday and early afternoon
3 late afternoon
4 just after sunset
5 at night.

The Koran itself, although exhorting Muslims to pray, does not lay down the five daily times of prayer, but this practice is so firmly entrenched in Islam that Muhammad probably instituted it himself. In Muslim countries a man called a muezzin calls the people to prayer with these words, known as the Adhan:

'God is most Great' (four times)
'I bear witness that nothing deserves to be worshipped except God' (twice)
'I bear witness that Muhammad is the Messenger of God' (twice)
'Come to prayer' (twice)
'Come to what is good for you' (twice)
'God is most great' (twice)
'There is no god but God' (once)

So every day a Muslim sets aside regular times for prayer, even though they are fairly short periods each time. To pray is the first thing he does on getting up in the morning and the last thing he does before going to bed at night. Every day is seen to belong to God, and five times a day he must turn to God to recognise that he could not live without him and to draw strength from God to lead a good life.

8

Fig.3. These diagrams show the different bodily positions that Muslims take up when they pray. They are in sequence, except that (1) is repeated after (2) and (5) and (6) are done twice. It is important for Muslims that they involve both their minds and bodies in worship.

9

Muslims believe in making careful preparations before coming to God in prayer, just as we should take special care if we were to visit an important person. It is their way of showing their respect for God whom Muslims believe to be most great and far more important than any human being. So they must consciously intend to pray and be fully aware of what they are doing. They must also be clean in body and dress because in these prayers Muslims bring their minds and bodies to worship God. They believe that God created the whole man and therefore the whole man must worship him. There are detailed rules laid down to make sure that Muslims wash themselves properly before prayer. These involve a careful and thorough washing of the hands, mouth, nose, face and arms, all three times over; and the washing of the head, ears and feet once (the exposed parts of the body which get dirty quickly).

Such cleanliness shows respect for God and recognises that he is concerned with the body as well as the inner man. It also has hygienic advantages in hot countries where many Muslims live and where Islam began. Symbolically, the washing of the outside of the body represents the cleansing of the inner soul from sin. One Muslim tradition compares prayer to a stream in which a person bathes five times a day and so becomes spotlessly clean; for it is believed that God will wash away people's faults when they come to him in prayer. From this point of view, it is interesting to note that Muslims must still perform most of the motions of washing, using dust or sand, if there is no water available for a proper wash.

Once they have washed, Muslims cover their heads before praying. The men often wear a small round hat and the women cover themselves from head to foot, showing only their faces and hands. Now that he is ready, the Muslim simply has to find a clean place in which to pray. He does not have to go to a special holy place because God is thought to be everywhere. Even if he were out in the street he could roll out his prayer mat, take off his shoes, face the direction of Mecca and then begin his prayers. Most Muslims prefer to pray in a mosque or in their own homes with the whole family.

The prayers themselves consist of set words and alternative passages, mostly taken from their Holy Book, the Koran. One of the most famous prayers is the first chapter of the Koran, called the Opening:

In the name of Allah, the Compassionate, the Merciful.
Praise be to Allah, Lord of the Creation.
The Compassionate, the Merciful,
King of Judgement-day!
You alone we worship, and to You alone
we pray for help.
Guide us to the straight path

The path of those whom You have favoured,
Not of those who have incurred Your wrath,
Nor of those who have gone astray.

As he recites all the prayers, the Muslim goes through a series of motions which consist of standing, bowing and prostrating himself to God (see Fig.3). In this way the Muslim surrenders his whole self, body and mind, to God. The prayers end with him sitting back on his heels and turning his head first to the right and then to the left. In this way he remembers all his Muslim brothers wherever they are in the world and says:

'Peace be on you and Allah's blessings.'

The whole sequence of movements and words is called a rakah and it will be repeated between two and four times depending on the time of day. For example, the prayers performed after midday usually consist of four rakahs, except on a Friday when most Muslim men gather at the mosque for prayers and they are shortened to two rakahs to allow time for a sermon.

Generally then, the prayer sessions do not last long and the preparations become very quick with practice. What is important is that a Muslim is constantly reminded of God throughout the day. There are some Muslims, however, who find it very difficult to set aside the right times for prayer. In Muslim countries everything comes to a stop at these times, but it is not so easy for Muslim immigrants in other places who may be working on a factory assembly line, serving in a shop or teaching in a school. For these people a compromise must be made and they have to save most of their prayers for the evening when together they take about half an hour.

So far we have been speaking of salat, the obligatory prayers, but many Muslims will also pray privately to God whenever they want to.

Make sure you know
1 the first words a Muslim ever hears
2 how many times a day Muslims have to pray
3 all the preparations they must make before they pray

See if you understand
4 why Muslims pray so often
5 why they wash themselves before prayer

Issues to discuss
6 Why do you think Muslims are taught that prayer is good for them (in the call to prayer)?

7 Bearing in mind the importance Muslims place on the use of the body in prayer, consider whether some bodily positions are more helpful for prayer than others, and how far such positions can express what the prayers are about.

4 Charity

From his early years Muhammad learnt that life was hard. He never saw his father who died before he was born, and his mother died when he was only six years old. As an orphan he was cared for by other members of his family within his tribe: first by his grandfather and then his uncle. These early experiences shaped Muhammad's character. As a poor boy he realised that he would have to work hard if he was to get on in life. It may also have been his early hardships which gave him a deep compassion for all who were in need: orphans, widows, women, the poor, the sick and even dumb animals. In one Hadith he says:

'One who manages the affairs of the widow and the needy is like one who exerts himself hard in the way of God...'

In his attitude to the poor, Muhammad was living up to what he believed to be God's will. The Koran frequently urges generosity towards the needy. It sees man's duty to God as inseparable from his duty to his fellow man: you worship God not just by prayer but by the whole way in which you live. The Koran says:

'The righteous man is he who believes in Allah and the Last Day...who for the love of Allah gives his wealth to his kinsfolk, to the orphans, to the needy, to the wayfarers and to the beggars, and for the redemption of captives; who attends to his prayers and pays the alms-tax.' (*Chapter 2 verse 177*)

In the phrase 'attend to your prayers and pay the alms-tax', which is repeated several times in this chapter of the Koran, we see that charity is as much a religious duty as saying your prayers.

The alms-tax, or the Zakat, is basically two and a half per cent of earnings, which all Muslims must pay to charity. Muhammad levied this tax in the first Islamic state, over which he ruled. It was used at that time to support his followers who had left their homes and possessions to be with him and were therefore destitute. So Muhammad encouraged the richer people to give some of their money to help the poor. Muslims are still obliged to pay this tax and it is the third pillar of Islam. They believe that the ideal state is where all men recognise God as their head and each man as their

Fig.4. All Muslims must give a set proportion of their incomes to charity once a year. This helps to bring the rich and poor closer together. Sometimes it is collected by the state and sometimes it is given directly to the poor. This picture shows the Zakat box at the London Central Mosque where local Muslims can leave their donations.

brother. With this bond between them they are bound to help each other.

The word 'Zakat' literally means 'purification'. Muslims believe that by giving away a certain amount of their money they are purifying the rest of their wealth to use as they like. Islam does not teach that it is wrong to own money or that everyone should have equal shares. It encourages people to work hard and live honestly, and if God blesses their labours with rewards, then they should thank God and enjoy their wealth. But in thanking God, they are recognising that all things come from him and, just as God has been generous to them, so they should be generous to their fellow men, especially those most in need. Equally they should never use their wealth to harm another person. Nor should they just sit back and live off their wealth by investing it, but should work for their money. There are also rules about inheritance in the Koran. These make sure that, when a person dies, his wealth is divided up among members of his family rather than letting one or two individuals amass great wealth without earning it.

In Saudi Arabia, where Islamic laws are imposed, part of the Zakat is collected as the normal income tax and used by the state for social services. In Pakistan it is levied by the government on all Muslims but is distinct from the income tax. However, Shi'a Muslims have always insisted that giving to charity should be a personal matter and not organised by the state. Many other Muslims now live in countries which do not have Islamic laws; these people have to pay the normal taxes of their country as well as making sure that they give the required amount to charity.

The alms-tax does not ask people to give away very much and many Muslims give much more. The very poor people are not asked to pay Zakat, for they are the ones to whom it is given. The real importance of Zakat lies in the fact that every Muslim is forced to recognise his responsibility to his fellow Muslim. This attitude extends across national boundaries so that rich Muslim countries often help poorer Muslims elsewhere.

Make sure you know
1 how much a Muslim must pay for Zakat
2 what the money is used for

See if you understand
3 why all Muslims must pay the alms-tax
4 why it is called 'purification'
5 why some Muslim countries collect this as a state tax

Issues to discuss
6 How far do you think Islam has the right solution to the

problems caused by the unequal distribution of wealth in the world?

7 Why does Islam encourage generosity; and do you consider this to be a virtue?

5 Family life

As Muhammad grew up he became a trader like his uncle and like many other Arabs of his time. Arabia has always been a dry land of deserts where very little grows; but there was a living to be made by transporting goods from places like India and Africa, across Arabia to the Mediterranean lands further north (see Fig.1 on page 2). Because of the harsh conditions, the traders travelled together, carrying their exotic silks, spices and precious stones from the East on the backs of camels, and returning with food.

On these long, slow journeys across vast stretches of desert Muhammad would have seen the lights of isolated monasteries flickering in the night. He would have been told that Christian monks lived there. They were people who had given up everything to devote themselves to God, for in becoming a monk, a Christian took the three vows of poverty, chastity and obedience. Although Muhammad respected their dedication to God, he might have wondered if this were really the best way to serve God.

Muhammad himself never followed this particular religious way; in fact there are no monks in Islam. He came to believe that people should use properly all that God has given them: their money, their sexuality and their own minds. He did not think that God wanted people to give up these things in following him.

Islam teaches that sex is a good thing, but recognises that it is a powerful force which needs to be kept within its proper limits. Islam only allows sex within marriage. Men and women are taught to behave modestly in public so that they do not entice each other sexually. It is for this reason that many Muslim women cover themselves up in public, wearing long robes and veils across their faces (see Fig.5). The Koran says:

> Enjoin believing men to turn their eyes away from temptation and to restrain their carnal desires. This will make their lives purer. Allah has knowledge of all their actions.
>
> Enjoin believing women to turn their eyes away from temptation and to preserve their chastity; to cover their adornments (except such as are normally displayed); to draw their veils over their bosoms and not to reveal their finery except

Fig. 5. Islam teaches both men and women to behave modestly in public. For this reason many Muslim women veil themselves to cover up their faces as well as their bodies; but not all Muslims interpret the Koranic instructions in this way.

to their husbands...(The passage continues to list other members of the family) (*Chapter 24 verses 30–31*)

Muhammad believed marriage and family life were very important. When he became a religious leader later on in his life he encouraged the young men to marry so that they would be using their sexuality properly. The practice of polygamy was also allowed to continue. This is when a man has more than one wife. Muhammad himself had ten wives in all. Polygamy was important in the Arabia of Muhammad's day since many men were killed in battle. The women were left at home with the children and were dependent on the men for their support. The Koran states that a Muslim may take up to four wives as long as he treats them all equally and some wealthy Muslims, even today, do this in countries where it is permitted. However, elsewhere in the Koran it says:

Try as you may, you cannot treat all your wives impartially. (*Chapter 4 verse 129*)

This seems to warn people off polygamy and in practice the vast majority of Muslims have always been monogamous (i.e. having only one wife).

Marriage and family life are very important in Islam. Traditionally the man's duty is to go out to work to support the family, and the woman's duty is to bring up her children as well as possible. The father takes all the main decisions, while the mother is important within the home and her wishes must be respected by her children. All this is seen to be the natural order of things and in accordance with how God intended men and women to live.

Because of the importance of marriage, it has always been the custom in Islam for marriages to be arranged by the parents. This is very different from love-marriages in the West where young people go out with members of the opposite sex until two of them decide to get married. In Islam the first moves are made by the parents of the boy who look out for a suitable wife for him. They then approach the girl's parents and if the match is approved of they arrange for the boy and girl to meet. The boy and girl must both agree to it before getting married, although it may be that the girl feels obliged to do as her father suggests, especially if she is engaged when she is only in her early teens. Either way, they do not expect to fall in love before marriage. There is the feeling that love must be worked at and if they are committed to each other and supported by their families, love will grow between them.

It is interesting to note that there are fewer divorces in arranged marriages than in love matches. Islam does not like divorce but it is allowed, for it is recognised that two people may not be able to get on together.

The Prophet said: 'Never did God allow anything more hateful to him than divorce.'

The Koran lays down firm rules to make sure that the wife and children are not simply cast off and left destitute. Yet the fact remains that divorce is easier for a man than for a woman since the law courts regard women as more impulsive and irrational than men. Also, many Muslim women are financially dependent on their husbands, and would not want to leave their children whom the father has the right to keep.

Make sure you know
1 what is meant by polygamy

See if you understand

2 why there are no Muslim monks or nuns

3 why Muhammad encouraged people to get married

Issues to discuss

4 Do you think there are good reasons for arguing that sex should be confined to marriage, as Muslims do?

5 How far do you agree with Muslims that a man's place is out at work and a woman's place is in the home?

6 Can you think of any reasons why arranged marriages, such as are found amongst Muslims, often survive longer than love matches?

6 Fasting

In the previous chapter we saw how Islam helps men and women to live as naturally as possible. It does not generally make the sort of excessive demands on its followers as were accepted by monks in other religions. So it is perhaps surprising to find one practice in Islam which is very much in line with the kind of extreme discipline of monks and nuns. I am referring to the fourth pillar of Islam: fasting, or sawm.

To fast means to go without food for a time. Muslims can fast voluntarily if they want to for any reason, and Mondays and Thursdays are popular days for this as there is the tradition that this is what Muhammad himself did. But *all* adult Muslims are obliged to fast each year during the whole of their ninth month, called Ramadan. This is laid down in the Koran which says that during this month Muhammad first began to receive the words of God. So one of the reasons for the fast is to commemorate this event. Other reasons which Muslims give for this fast show that religious discipline is seen to be useful as long as excessive demands are only made for set periods. The Koran says:

> Believers, fasting is decreed for you as it was decreed for those before you; perchance you will guard yourselves against evil. (*Chapter 2 verse 183*)

By fasting in this way, Muslims are asked to give up something for God. So they are testing their powers of endurance as well as their faith in God. They are learning to control their bodies for the sake of their religion and in this way they recognise that they do not just have bodies, but also souls. It also has practical purposes. By fasting, Muslims are finding out what it feels like to be hungry and will therefore be more sympathetic towards the poor who cannot afford to buy enough food. It may also be that one day they themselves will be poor and they will have already learnt to bear the pain of hunger. Finally, as with all the five pillars of Islam, it brings Muslims closer together in brotherhood, for at this time each year *all* Muslims are going through exactly the same experience.

The rules for this fast are laid down in the Koran and must be followed by all Muslims once they have reached the age of ten,

Days	Ramadan	July/Aug	LONDON		BIRMINGHAM			BRADFORD			BRIGHTON			BRISTOL		
			Begin	Ends	Begin	Sunrise	Ends	Begin	Sunrise	Ends	Begin	Sunrise	Ends	Begin	Sunrise	Ends
Sun	1st	13 July	3.06	9.13	2.56	5.00	9.25	2.43	4.53	9.32	3.12	5.02	9.10	3.16	5.09	9.23
Mon	2nd	14	3.08	9.12	2.58	5.01	9.24	2.45	4.54	9.31	3.14	5.03	9.09	3.18	5.10	9.22
Tues	3rd	15	3.10	9.11	3.00	5.03	9.23	2.47	4.55	9.30	3.16	5.04	9.08	3.20	5.11	9.21
Wed.	4th	16	3.12	9.10	3.02	5.04	9.22	2.50	4.57	9.29	3.18	5.05	9.07	3.22	5.12	9.20
Thur	5th	17	3.14	9.09	3.04	5.05	9.21	2.53	4.58	9.27	3.20	5.07	9.06	3.24	5.13	9.19
Fri	6th	18	3.16	9.08	3.06	5.07	9.20	2.56	4.59	9.26	3.22	5.08	9.05	3.26	5.15	9.18
Sat	7th	19	3.18	9.07	3.08	5.08	9.18	2.59	5.01	9.25	3.24	5.09	9.04	3.28	5.16	9.16
Sun	8th	20	3.20	9.06	3.10	5.09	9.17	3.02	5.02	9.23	3.26	5.10	9.03	3.30	5.17	9.15
Mon	9th	21	3.22	9.05	3.12	5.11	9.16	3.05	5.05	9.21	3.28	5.12	9.02	3.32	5.19	9.14
Tues	10th	22	3.25	9.03	3.15	5.12	9.14	3.07	5.05	9.21	3.30	5.13	9.00	3.35	5.20	9.13
Wed	11th	23	3.27	9.02	3.18	5.13	9.13	3.10	5.07	9.19	3.32	5.14	8.59	3.37	5.21	9.11
Thur	12th	24	3.29	9.01	3.20	5.15	9.12	3.13	5.08	9.18	3.34	5.16	8.58	3.39	5.23	9.10
Fri	13th	25	3.31	8.59	3.22	5.16	9.10	3.16	5.10	9.16	3.36	5.17	8.56	3.41	5.24	9.09
Sat	14th	26	3.33	8.58	3.25	5.18	9.09	3.19	5.11	9.14	3.38	5.18	8.55	3.43	5.25	9.07
Sun	15th	27	3.35	8.56	3.27	5.19	9.07	3.21	5.13	9.13	3.40	5.20	8.54	3.45	5.27	9.06
Mon	16th	28	3.37	8.55	3.29	5.21	9.06	3.23	5.15	9.11	3.42	5.21	8.52	3.47	5.28	9.04
Tues	17th	29	3.40	8.53	3.32	5.22	9.04	3.26	5.16	9.09	3.44	5.23	8.51	3.50	5.30	9.02
Wed	18th	30	3.42	8.52	3.35	5.24	9.02	3.29	5.18	9.08	3.46	5.24	8.49	3.52	5.31	9.01
Thu	19th	31	3.45	8.50	3.38	5.25	9.01	3.32	5.20	9.06	3.48	5.25	8.48	3.55	5.33	9.00
Fri	20th	1 Aug	3.47	8.48	3.40	5.27	8.59	3.35	5.21	9.04	3.50	5.27	8.46	3.57	5.34	8.58
Sat	21st	2	3.50	8.47	3.43	5.29	8.57	3.38	5.23	9.02	3.52	5.28	8.44	4.00	5.36	8.56
Sun	22nd	3	3.52	8.45	3.45	5.30	8.56	3.41	5.25	9.00	3.54	5.30	8.43	4.03	5.37	8.55
Mon	23rd	4	3.55	8.43	3.48	5.32	8.54	3.44	5.26	8.59	3.57	5.31	8.41	4.05	5.39	8.53
Tues	24th	5	3.57	8.42	3.51	5.33	8.52	3.47	5.28	8.57	3.59	5.33	8.39	4.07	5.40	8.51
Wed	25th	6	3.59	8.40	3.54	5.35	8.50	3.49	5.30	8.55	4.01	5.34	8.38	4.09	5.42	8.49
Thu	26th	7	4.01	8.38	3.56	5.37	8.48	3.51	5.31	8.53	4.03	5.36	8.36	4.11	5.43	8.48
Fri	27th	8	4.03	8.36	3.59	5.38	8.46	3.53	5.33	8.51	4.05	5.37	8.34	4.13	5.45	8.46
Sat	28th	9	4.05	8.34	4.01	5.40	8.44	3.56	5.35	8.49	4.07	5.39	8.32	4.15	5.46	8.44
Sun	29th	10	4.08	8.33	4.03	5.42	8.42	3.58	5.37	8.47	4.10	5.40	8.30	4.18	5.48	8.42
Mon	30th	11	4.10	8.31	4.06	5.43	8.40	4.00	5.38	8.45	4.12	5.42	8.29	4.20	5.50	8.40

Fig.6. Muslims fast during the month of Ramadan from daybreak to sunset. They need different calendars each year, like this one, to tell them the exact times of the fast for where they live.

although usually children from about six years old will try to join in. For the twenty-nine or thirty days of Ramadan no food, drink, smoking or sex are allowed and no evil thoughts, words or actions. This begins each day at dawn and lasts right through until sunset. So Muslims need to know the correct times of the fast for where they live and calendars are issued for this purpose (see Fig.6). Obviously the fasts are most demanding for those who live in hot countries for they are expected to go right through the heat of the day without a drink; and during the summer the days are longest. The Muslim calendar is worked out according to the moon rather than the sun so that the Muslim year is eleven days shorter than the Western year. This means that Ramadan comes at a different time each year and is sometimes in the summer and sometimes in the winter.

As you can imagine, the fast is very demanding on Muslims and slows them down at work and school. This can cause difficulties if they are not living in a Muslim country. However, anyone who is too weak to fast is not expected to do so. This includes young children, the sick, the elderly, pregnant or nursing mothers, travellers and soldiers. If possible they will make up for it later.

After sunset there is usually a party atmosphere with the children going round the streets with brightly coloured glass lanterns, singing songs and eating sweets. Their parents will probably be entertaining or visiting friends and relatives. They will send food to their neighbours, particularly the poor, so that everyone can join in the celebrations. So from giving up their food during the day, they have learnt to give up some of their food for the poor during the night. As well as the first big meal when they break their fast, there is a light snack before the fast begins again. This is best eaten in the very early morning and usually consists of yoghurt, cheese or honey. But those who are not sure of waking up early enough eat it before going to bed because once the first light of day appears the fast begins once more.

You can imagine the tremendous rejoicing when this whole month of fasting comes to an end. One of the two major festivals of Islam is celebrated at this time: the Festival of Fast-Breaking, called Eid-ul-Fitr which means the Little Festival. It is especially popular with the children. It begins with the whole family attending a morning service in the mosque, their place of worship. Sometimes there have to be several services, one after the other, to accommodate everyone as most mosques are fairly small since usually only the men attend them in any number. In hot countries a sheet may be spread out on the ground outside the mosque to cope with the overspill. Everyone dresses up in their best clothes and after the service they visit their friends and relatives, exchanging presents, cards (see Fig.11 on page 43) and sweets. The special dessert prepared for the occasion is a sweet pudding containing dates and milk, which recalls the desert days of the Prophet. It is a time when people have been through a lot together and now they are looking forward to enjoying God's blessings until Ramadan comes round once more.

Make sure you know
1 when Muslims have to fast
2 what they have to give up
3 what happens when the fast is over

See if you understand
4 why a particular month was chosen for the fast
5 what Muslims hope to achieve by fasting

Issues to discuss

6 Would you agree with Muslims that it is sometimes useful to go without things?

7 Muslims emphasise the fellowship they feel with each other when fasting. Do you think it is true that people often become more friendly when sharing together in some adversity? Can you think of some examples?

7 Belief in One God

On Muhammad's travels as a trader, he would have come into contact with foreigners who had different beliefs and religions from his own, and perhaps he picked up some of their ideas. But he would have been influenced most by other Arabs who spoke his own language and who sat around the camp fires in the evenings telling their tales. Some of them belonged to tribes which had been converted to Judaism, and others were Christians. Both of these religions are monotheistic; that means they believe there is only one God. There were also Arabs who called themselves Hanifs which means those 'who are inclined' to believe in one God.

When Muhammad returned from each journey to his home in the city of Mecca, he must have wondered if the people who worshipped only one God were not right after all. The Jews, the Christians and the Hanifs each had their own name for God, but they recognised that they were referring to the same God. They believed that there was only the one God who was lord of all the world, and indeed of the whole universe, whereas in Mecca polytheism flourished. Polytheism means that people worship many gods. Mecca was not only the main trading centre of Arabia at that time but also a religious centre to which people came on pilgrimage. The main shrine was called the Kaaba and this building housed three hundred and sixty idols—man-made images of the gods and goddesses that people worshipped.

Later in his life Muhammad was to destroy all these idols and teach the people that there existed only one God. The name he used for God was Allah which is simply the Arabic for 'the God'. In fact this name was already used by the people of Mecca. Muhammad's own father had been called 'Abd-Allah' which means 'slave of Allah'. Allah had probably been the name of the supreme, remote god of the Meccans. Muhammad was making the point that they must worship Allah alone. There could not also be different gods for each tribe, or gods specially to help them win their battles, or goddesses to bring them and their animals fertility; nor could there be good and bad spirits which lived in the wind, the hills, the caves, the wells and other places. He taught that there was only one God who was all powerful and therefore in charge of all these things. He

The ninetynine Attributes Of God

Fig.7. The Koran speaks of ninety-nine attributes of God, known by Muslims as the Beautiful Names.

regarded idolatry as the greatest of all sins since this was the worship of idols and other gods rather than the one true God.

This belief in the oneness of God is the most important belief in Islam and is the first pillar. The short declaration of Muslim beliefs begins: 'There is no God but Allah', and the most important verses in the Koran are:

Say: 'Allah is One, the Eternal God. He begot none, nor was He begotten. None is equal to Him.' (*Chapter 112*)

This means that God is believed to have existed always and that there never was a time when there was no God. He was not made by some greater power, nor has he given birth to lesser gods. He alone is God. In the Koran he is called The One.

There are other names given to God, mostly found in the Koran, which help us to build up a picture of the God Muslims believe in and worship. These are known as the Ninety-nine Beautiful Names (see Fig.7). Some Muslims use strings of prayer beads called subhas with ninety-nine beads on them to remind them of these different aspects of God.

He is called the Lord, the High, the Mighty, the Great, the King of Kingship, and we are told in the Koran: 'He is over all things supreme'. All of these things emphasise God's power for he is far greater than man. Muslims believe that he is even greater than anything they can imagine and they are forbidden to make any images of him since nothing made by man could possibly measure up to God himself. There are no Muslim statues or pictures of God or any other symbols to stand for him. God in himself remains a mystery to Muslims and they believe it is only because he has sent down his words through his prophets that mere human beings can know anything about him at all.

He is called the Creator, the Life-Giver and the Provider. These names tell us that God is believed to have made everything in heaven and on earth, and that the existence of everyone and everything depends upon him. Muslims therefore accept everything which happens in life as being the will of Allah, whether it is good or bad. They believe God sends bad things to punish the wicked or to test the faithful.

He is also called the Kindly and the Forgiver. Indeed, every chapter of the Koran contains the phrase:

In the name of Allah, the Compassionate, the Merciful.

These are the opening words of every chapter except one. Muslims say that God is willing to forgive the wrongs of the believers who turn to him. Yet we also find him called the Knowing One, the Reckoner and the Bringer-Down. These names show that God is also believed to be a fearful judge who knows us better than we know ourselves and who will bring the non-believers what they deserve.

This is the God that Muhammad came to believe in and that Islam teaches.

Make sure you know
1 which religions are monotheistic
2 what polytheism means
3 what an idol is
4 how many 'Beautiful Names' Muslims have for God

See if you understand
5 why Muhammad called God 'Allah'
6 why Muslims are strictly forbidden to use any images in their religion
7 why Muslims believe that everything comes from God, whether it is good or bad

Issues to discuss
8 Why do you think that many people, like the Muslims, believe that there is a supreme Being in charge of the world?
9 How satisfactory do you find the Muslim answer to the problem of suffering in the world?

8 The Holy Koran

When Muhammad was twenty-five he married Khadija, the rich widow who owned the camel caravan on which he worked. He remained happily married to her until she died twenty-five years later and only then took a number of other wives. Now that he was married to her, he no longer had any money worries and, although he continued to work, he could spend more time pursuing his other interests and it became clear that he was a deeply religious man. He used to go off alone into the desert to pray. There was one cave in particular that he used to climb up to, just outside Mecca, on Mount Hira. From there he would watch the beauty of the sky at sunset, splashed with colour. He would gaze in wonder at the star-spangled night sky, and see with relief the first grey light of dawn after the long, cold vigil of the night.

It is interesting to reflect upon the fact that people of all religions are drawn by the deserts. These are places where they can be perfectly alone with their thoughts, undisturbed by the bustle of worldly affairs. It is also the vastness of the desert which brings home to men and women their own smallness and frailty. In such conditions it is not hard to feel that you are totally dependent upon God and to be struck with awe and wonder at his creation. Perhaps it was his own experiences of feeling close to God on such occasions that led Muhammad to emphasise that each individual must be responsible for coming to God himself. There are no priests or specially holy people in Islam, no-one to act as a go-between to pray to God for the people.

Some years later, when Muhammad was forty years old, something very dramatic happened to him one night on Mount Hira. Muslims date this event as the 27th. Ramadan and celebrate it during the last ten days of that month. It is referred to in the Koran as the Night of Power. Here in the stillness and enveloping darkness of the desert night Muhammad had a vision of the Archangel Gabriel bringing him the words of God and saying:

Recite in the name of your Lord who created, created man from clots of blood! (*Chapter 96 verse 1*)

Fig.8. The Koran is the holy book of Muslims. It is in Arabic which is written from right to left, beginning at the top of the page. This page is from a Koran of the 12th. or 13th. century C.E. It shows the care which is taken to make the writing beautiful, with geometric decorations.

At first Muhammad himself could hardly believe it was true, but after this first shattering experience came others which continued to occur throughout the rest of his life. And although many people thought he was mad, it is interesting that those who knew him best supported him, his wife Khadija becoming his first convert.

Muslims believe that it was in this way that God gradually revealed his law to Muhammad. He repeated everything to his listeners who learnt it and wrote it down. These prophecies were carefully collected together very soon after Muhammad's death and recorded in the Koran so that Muslims have no doubt as to

30

their genuineness and correctness. Great care was always taken when making new copies of the Koran so that today Muslims have the same pure text that has been passed down for centuries.

Muhammad is never spoken of as the writer of the Koran, for Muslims do not think that he composed the words himself but that he was simply the mouthpiece through which God spoke his own words. Muhammad was simply commanded to recite the words which God gave him. The word 'Koran' means 'recitation'.

Since the Koran was revealed to Muhammad in Arabic, it has remained in that language as it is feared that translations might alter the original meaning (see Fig.8). Most Muslims therefore learn the Koran by heart in Arabic, starting this at about the age of four when they attend special schools at their local mosque, the religious centre. The Koran is fairly easy to remember because it is written in verses of short lines which end in rhyming words. Muslims learn how the Arabic should be chanted and they regard the Koran as unsurpassable in its beauty as a work of literature. Altogether the Koran has over 6,000 verses and is divided into 114 chapters, or suras. Each of these chapters has a special title. Muslims divide up the Koran into thirty parts so that it can be recited completely in their worship each month. Again we see that the title 'Koran' or 'Recitation', is appropriate.

The Koran is such a holy book that Muslims always treat it with great respect. They must wash before touching it, as for prayer, and they will usually keep it on a high shelf when it is not being read, with nothing standing on top of it.

The Koran is believed to be the final revelation of God's will to mankind, providing the guidelines for the perfect human community. The Koran says:

This day I have perfected your religion for you and completed My favour to you. I have chosen Islam to be your faith.
(*Chapter 5 verse 3b*)

It is said to contain God's law, but this does not mean that there are simply lists of rules, instead there are guidelines and warnings as to how to live in God's way. Using the Koran as its base, Islam has developed ways of working out how God's law is to be applied in each new situation.

Make sure you know
1 what event is commemorated on the 27th. Ramadan
2 what the Holy Book of Islam is called

See if you understand
3 why there are no Muslim priests
4 why their holy book must remain in Arabic

Issues to discuss

5 Muhammad had a religious experience on Mount Hira. Why do you think people often feel closer to God on mountains and in deserts? Are there any other places where you might expect people to have similar feelings?

6 The Koran is believed to contain the very *words* of God. How is this different from regarding a holy book as the *word* of God? (Consider whether the words or the people are inspired.)

7 Do you agree with the reasons given by Islam for *not* having clergy?

9 Mosques

Muhammad felt compelled to preach to his own people what he believed God had made known to him. He called them to live in God's way: worshipping the one God as Lord of all and living good, honest lives in harmony with each other.

Muhammad had a difficult task for the Arabs did not want to listen when he told them that they were wrong to worship idols. No one likes to have his deep-rooted beliefs challenged. No one likes to be shaken out of his cosy, traditional way of life. What is more, many people in Mecca made money from their religion: their shrine drew large crowds of people and this was good for business.

Muhammad's persistence eventually brought him persecution and after ten difficult years he was forced to flee for his life. He rode over 200 miles north-east across the desert to a town where he had been invited to live. It was called Yathrib but it soon became known as Medina-al-Nabi (the 'the City of the Prophet'), or simply Medina (see Fig.2 on page 5). There he settled with the Emigrants, the believers who had come with him from Mecca. He lived out the rest of his life in Medina ruling the people there and making further converts to Islam who were known as his Helpers.

This emigration was extremely important in the history of Islam. In one sense it was the beginning of Islam. For Islam does not just consist of religious beliefs and worship but is a whole way of life, lived according to the laws which God made known to Muhammad. It was not until Muhammad settled in Medina, where his leadership was accepted by all the tribes there, that he was able to put these laws into effect. So Muslims date their calendar from this event. What was the 16th. July 622 C.E. (Common Era) or A.D. (Anno Domini—in the year of the Lord i.e. Jesus Christ) became for them the first day of the year 1 A.H. (Anno Hegirae—in the year of the Hijra, or Emigration).

When Muhammad first reached Medina he let his camel stop where it wanted and there he set about building his house and the first Muslim place of worship, the first mosque. The word 'mosque' means a place of 'prostration', for it is here that Muslims kneel down and bow their heads to the ground in prostration to God (see Fig.3(5) on page 9). As was explained in Chapter 3 on

Fig.9. This is the London Central Mosque in Regent's Park. This new building is the grandest mosque in Britain and was opened in 1977.

Prayer, it is not necessary to go to this special building to pray; indeed Muhammad said that the whole world was God's mosque, for people could pray to him anywhere. But mosques have always been built by Muslim communities as their religious centres where the weekly service is held on Fridays, where the people can gather to celebrate their festivals and where children can learn to recite the Koran. Usually these buildings are put up especially for the purpose, but sometimes Muslim immigrants have had to use a room in their own houses as a mosque or take over existing buildings like disused churches.

Since Muhammad first built his mosque at Medina, many thousands of other mosques have been built all over the world. Some of them have been very small, plain buildings; others magnificent feats of architecture (see Fig.9 and Fig.14 on page 56); and all of them have been influenced by the types of buildings which already existed in the countries in which Muslims have lived. But the basic essentials of any mosque are very simple.

Outside, it must provide somewhere for the Muslims to wash

themselves before they pray and somewhere to leave their shoes which they take off before they go inside. The washing facilities may take the form of an open-air pool, a fountain, a separate building with ladies' and gentlemen's cloakrooms or simply some jars of water. Also on the outside of most mosques is built at least one tall tower called a minaret. It is from the top of the minaret, standing out on a balcony, that the muezzin calls the people to prayer.

Inside, the mosque is almost bare. There are no seats because space must be left for worshippers to go through the various positions of prayer, which include sitting on the ground (see Fig.3 on page 9). Since they worship in bare feet, the floor is normally carpeted. The only piece of furniture is a pulpit from which the Friday sermon is preached. This is simply a raised, wooden platform at the top of at least three steps, though in large mosques it is much higher than this so that the preacher can be seen and heard clearly. There might also be some sort of screen to separate the women from the men; or it may be that a balcony for the women is part of the building. The women, if they attend the mosque at all, always stand behind the men. The reason given for this is that neither sex will distract the other and the men will not embarrass the women by looking at them as they go through the positions of prayer. The only other thing to look for in a mosque is the small alcove, called a mihrab, in the centre of the far wall. The purpose of this is to point the Muslims in the direction of Mecca since, you will remember, they face Mecca when they pray.

There are never any statues or pictures of any kind in a mosque. This was strictly forbidden by Muhammad who knew all about the dangers of idolatry and was afraid that people would go back to worshipping the statues instead of God himself. Muslims are never allowed to draw either people or animals for this reason and therefore they have developed an art form of intricate patterns. These exquisite decorations can be seen in some of the wealthier mosques, often done on tiles or sculpted into the plaster. In most mosques though the only decoration is words from the Koran written on the walls. This Arabic writing can look very beautiful and is an art form in itself (see Fig.8 on page 30).

Make sure you know
1 what A.H. stands for in a Muslim date
2 what mosques are used for
3 all the things you would find inside a mosque

See if you understand
4 why mosques are so called
5 why washing facilities have to be provided outside a mosque

Issues to discuss

6 Are there any advantages in having a special building in which to pray?

7 Do you think it is right to spend a lot of money on building a house of God?

10 Pilgrimage to Mecca

Once Muhammad had left Mecca for Medina, fighting broke out between the two cities and continued on and off for the next six years. Although the Muslims were greatly outnumbered, Muhammad proved himself to be a very able commander and they eventually got the upper hand.

It was very important to Muhammad that he should convert the Meccans to Islam because Mecca was already an ancient religious centre and this would make a big impact on all the surrounding Arab tribes which came to the city. For Arabs came to Mecca as pilgrims specially to visit the holy places there. So when the time was right, Muhammad advanced on the city with a huge army of 20,000. Mecca gave in without a fight. Here, eight years after he had fled for his life, Muhammad made peace with the Meccans, generously sparing the lives of his enemies and converting the city to Islam.

Muhammad's first act was to destroy all the idols of the Kaaba; but he did not destroy the great shrine itself, nor the other holy places in Mecca. He wanted Mecca to remain a religious centre, but from now on it would be the centre of Islam. He did not regard himself as starting a new religion, but rather as bringing people back to the true religion which God had begun to make known to them about 2,500 years before. So he set about restoring the original meaning to these holy places. We find that many of them are connected with Abraham who is regarded as an important prophet in Islam because he was the first person to worship the one God. Tradition has it that the Arabs are descended from Abraham's son Ishmael, and the Jews from his son Isaac.

Mecca is still the centre of Islam and still a great place of pilgrimage, attracting over a million Muslims each year. The city is so holy for Muslims that non-Muslims are not allowed to come within ten miles of it. They want people to come for religious reasons, not as tourists. Muslims can make a minor pilgrimage to Mecca whenever they want to, but the fifth pillar of Islam makes it a duty for all Muslims to go there on the Major Pilgrimage, called the Hajj, at least once in their life if they can possibly manage it.

Fig.10. The Kaaba inside the Grand Mosque at Mecca is the main shrine of Islam. More than a million pilgrims visit it each year. It is covered with a cloth which is made specially for it, the old one being cut up and given to the pilgrims.

The Koran says:

> Exhort all men to make the pilgrimage. (*Chapter 22 verse 27*)
> Pilgrimage to the House is a duty to Allah for all who can make the journey. (*Chapter 3 verse 97*)

The Arabic word 'Hajj' means 'to set out for a definite purpose'. The main purpose is to dedicate yourself totally to God. During this time the pilgrims forget all about their everyday lives. Before they start the pilgrimage the men must take off their ordinary clothes and dress identically in pilgrim robes. These consist of two white unsewn cotton sheets, one of which is tied round the waist, and the other thrown over the left shoulder, leaving the right arm and shoulder bare. Their heads are bare and so are their feet unless they want to wear backless sandals. There is no special dress for the women but they have to dress modestly, being draped from head to foot although their faces are left unveiled. Dressing in this way reminds the pilgrims that they are entering into a state of consecration. This means that they have dedicated themselves entirely to God. Whilst in this state they must not shave or have sex. They have set aside all their worldly wealth, comforts, family life, work, positions in society and nationality in order to devote themselves to God for as long as the pilgrimage lasts. This is expressed in the frequent cry of 'Labbaika' which means 'Doubly at your service, O God.'

The chief purpose of the Muslims' pilgrimage is to dedicate themselves to God, but there are other purposes too. By dressing and acting in exactly the same way, the unity of Muslims is shown. On pilgrimage no distinction is made between Muslims who in ordinary life may be important or unimportant, rich or poor, black or white. At this time more than at any other, Muslims are aware of their brotherhood, for they are all serving the one God. Another purpose is to visit the places around Mecca where the Prophet Muhammad himself once walked, and this is very exciting for them because it puts them in touch with the historical roots of their religion.

The Hajj is to be undertaken during the twelfth month of the Islamic year, the sacred month called Dhul-Hijja. The pilgrimage proper begins on the eighth day of the month and lasts three days, but most Muslims will have taken a lot of trouble to get there and usually stay longer than this. When they arrive they are taken to the various holy places in groups, led by a religious guide.

Usually the first thing a Muslim will want to see is the Kaaba. This huge, cube-shaped building stands in the centre of a large open-air courtyard inside the Great Mosque (see Fig.10). The Koran says that Abraham first built it, helped by his son Ishmael, and it was therefore the first house of God. It is now empty and the pilgrims do not go inside. In one of its walls, close to the ground, there is the famous Black Stone. This is believed to have come from heaven, and it may well be a meteorite. One legend says that it was originally white but has been turned black by people's sins. The wall around the Black Stone has been rubbed smooth by millions of hands touching it over the years. The pilgrims walk anti-clockwise round the Kaaba seven times as they say their prayers. They begin from the Black Stone and those nearest to it try to kiss or touch it, whilst those further away can only raise a hand towards it as they go by.

The next place they visit in Mecca is the passageway between two hills: Mount Safa and Mount Marwa. Traditionally it was here that Abraham was commanded by God to leave Hagar, his slave woman, and their son, Ishmael. At that time this was barren desert land and Hagar ran around frantically searching for water. When she came back to her young son she found that he had dug his heels into the ground and miraculously water had sprung up. The pilgrims re-enact this story by running seven times between the two hills and climbing each of them before going to the Zamzam well where they drink the water and buy containers of it to take back home with them.

On the eighth day of the month the pilgrims travel to Mount Arafat which is about thirteen miles from Mecca. Many will go on foot as part of their religious devotion. The plain around the mountain is filled with white tents as hundreds of thousands of Muslims gather there. The next day they climb Mount Arafat, known as the Mount of Mercy, to confess their sins to God, and join together in prayer. The Prophet said:

The best of prayers is the prayer of the day of Arafat.

That evening they leave Arafat and spend the night out under the stars at Muzdalifa, a place five miles on the way back to Mecca.

The next day they go on to Mina, a small village where there are three stone pillars and where they perform the ritual known as the stoning of the devil. They each throw seven pebbles at the pillars, shouting each time: 'In the name of God! Allah is almighty!' In this way they remember the story of how the Prophet Ishmael was tempted three times by the devil and drove him away by throwing stones at him. The pilgrims are showing that they too are rejecting evil.

Strictly speaking this is the last ritual that the pilgrims must perform but the next chapter will tell you more of what the pilgrims do.

Once a Muslim has been on the Hajj he is known as a Hajji and is given special respect in his community at home. He will tell the others all about it, helping them to share in the experience at second hand. For although every Muslim wants to get to Mecca, not everyone is able to do so. Some who are too poor to take a chartered flight to Arabia wait until they have retired and then set out on foot. For those who never make it, it is possible for others to do the pilgrimage on their behalf.

Make sure you know
1 the name of the central shrine of Islam
2 the name of Abraham's son from whom the Arabs are said to be descended
3 the name of the mountain where all the pilgrims gather for prayer

See if you understand

4 why all Muslims hope to go on the Major Pilgrimage
5 why they have to wear special clothes for it
6 why they 'stone the devil' at Mina

Issues to discuss

7 Try to imagine what a pilgrim would feel like when visiting the Muslim sacred places.
8 Do you think Islam is right to bar tourists from its holiest city?

11 Festivals

The two most important festivals in Islam are those which Muhammad himself started. In Chapter 6 we have already referred to the Festival of Fast Breaking, or the Little Festival, called Eid-ul-Fitr ('eid' meaning 'festival'). The other one is the Festival of Sacrifice, or the Great Festival, called Eid-ul-Adha. It comes at the end of the Major Pilgrimage, on the 10th. Dhul-Hijja.

When the pilgrims have finished the essential parts of the pilgrimage they remove their pilgrim clothes, wash, shave and cut their hair to show that they are no longer in the state of consecration. They have devoted themselves whole-heartedly to God for a few days and now they can relax together in thanksgiving to God.

The festival is held at Mina and begins with a big feast for which animals are sacrificed. Families which can afford it offer a lamb, sheep or goat, whilst seven families together may offer a cow or a camel. All animals which are to be eaten by Muslims are killed in a special way: prayers are said over them and the blood is drained away. You will see 'halal' food shops where Muslims buy all their meat, for this word means it is 'permitted' to them. At the festival only a third of the meat is kept by those who offer it, the rest being shared out amongst others, particularly the poor. For a religious sacrifice means giving up something of value for the sake of God and your fellow man.

This sacrifice of animals reminds Muslims of the story of how Abraham was commanded by God to sacrifice his son and how he was willing to obey God even to this extent. Then at the last moment God stopped him from killing the boy and gave him an animal to sacrifice instead. This represents the whole spirit of sacrifice which lies behind the pilgrimage. Muslims are taught that they must be prepared to give up everything for God. So after the tremendous demands of the pilgrimage, the Muslims rejoice together, sharing their food with each other. They usually relax in this way for three days before putting on their pilgrim clothes once more for a final visit to the Kaaba before they leave.

Meanwhile at home those who could not attend the pilgrimage itself this time will be celebrating the festival all the same and

Cover (right-hand page)

Inside (left-hand page)

الإمام الله عليك ورحمة السلام والبركة

BEST WISHES FOR THE HAPPY "EID"

Fig.11. Muslims send each other cards to celebrate festivals. They have Arabic writing and open from left to right.

43

sending each other cards (see Fig.11). Once again this emphasises the unity of all Muslims.

If pilgrims have the time and the money they may go on from Mecca to Medina, the city where the Prophet lived out the last ten years of his life and where he was buried. Some may also travel on to Jerusalem. This city is holy for Jews, Christians and Muslims. It is important for Muslims because the Koran says that Muhammad visited Jerusalem during the tenth year of his prophethood. He is said to have travelled in one night from the Kaaba in Mecca to the remains of the Jewish Temple in Jerusalem about 730 miles away.

> Glory be to Him who made His servants go by night from the Sacred Temple to the farther Temple whose surroundings We have blessed, that We might show him some of Our signs. (*Chapter 17 verse 1*)

Also in Jerusalem is the spectacular mosque called the Dome of the Rock. It was built during the first century of Islam and is the earliest existing monument of Muslim architecture. It is built over the rock from which Muhammad is supposed to have gone up to heaven on the night of his miraculous visit to Jerusalem. It is also believed that the five daily prayers of Islam were laid down during this night.

The Night of the Journey and the Ascension is remembered each year by Muslims. They celebrate it by reading the Koran and saying extra prayers on the night before the 27th. Rajab, their seventh month.

This is only one of the historical occasions which are commemorated in Islam. Another is the Day of the Hijra or Emigration, which is remembered on new year's day, the 1st. Muharram. They also celebrate Muhammad's birthday on the 12th. Rabi'ul-Awwal (he was born on 20th. August 570 C.E.) and the whole of this third month is considered sacred because of it. As Muhammad is regarded by Muslims as the last and greatest prophet, his birth is seen as the most important event in the history of the world. On this day Muslims gather to hear stories of the Prophet's life.

The only other historical event which is commemorated is Muhammad's call to prophecy on the Night of Power (Qadr) when he is believed to have first been given the words of the Koran by God. The chapter in the Koran called 'Qadr' says this:

> In the Name of Allah, the Compassionate, the Merciful
> We revealed the Koran on the Night of Qadr.
> Would that you knew what the Night of Qadr is like!
> Better is the Night of Qadr than a thousand months.
> On that night the angels and the Spirit by their Lord's
>   leave come down with His decrees.

That night is peace, till break of dawn. (*Chapter 97*)

So there are six annual celebrations: the two festivals which Muhammad himself started and the four historical events in the life of Muhammad which became fixed dates for Muslims to observe from soon after his death. The Shi'ites, however, have their own special festivals in addition to these. The most important is a ten day period of mourning when they re-enact the martyrdom of 'Ali's son, Husayn.

Apart from these, every Friday is important to Muslims as their holy day. It is called Yaum ul-Juma't which means Day of Assembly. Muslim men are obliged on this day to gather together for the midday prayers. Before gathering at their local mosque they will make themselves clean and tidy. There, one of their number will lead the prayers and preach a sermon to remind them of their religious duties and keep them in touch with the Islamic attitude to current affairs. This person is called an imam. He is not regarded as especially holy and may have no special training. He is simply someone who is respected by his fellow Muslims and who knows the Koran. After the service they all return to their work, for there is no day of rest in Islam. The Koran says:

Believers, when you are summoned to Friday prayers hasten to the remembrance of Allah and cease your trading. That would be best for you, if you but knew it. Then, when the prayers are ended, disperse and go in quest of Allah's bounty. Remember Allah always, so that you may prosper. (*Chapter 62 verses 9 – 10*)

Apart from these regular observances, there are of course special celebrations among Muslims as among all types of people: at the birth of a baby, at marriage and death. We shall be looking at the last of these in the next chapter.

Make sure you know
1 which festival is celebrated at the end of the pilgrimage
2 which are the four events in the life of Muhammad that are commemorated

See if you understand
3 why there are only two chief festivals in Islam
4 why it is said that the pilgrimage is a time of sacrifice
5 why Jerusalem is holy to Muslims

Issues to discuss
6 How important do you think it is to have a holy day each week?
   Notice that the Muslim holy day is not a day of rest and in most

respects is very similar to any other day of the week. Does this matter?

7 Are there any features of the Muslim festivals which are common to the way *you* celebrate important events?

12 Death

Once Mecca had been won over to Islam, Muhammad returned to his home in Medina where he was only to survive for another two years. In March 632 C.E. he visited Mecca for the last time to perform the Hajj. This is known as the Pilgrimage of Farewell for while he was on it he preached a sermon from Mount Arafat in which he made it clear that he knew he would soon die, and said goodbye to his followers. The following June he died of fever at the age of sixty-two.

Muhammad had always made it clear that Muslims were not to glorify him, a mere man, but were to worship God alone. When he died, Abu Bakr, his successor, said this:

If there are any among you who worshipped Muhammad, he is dead. But if it is God you worship, He lives forever.

One day death will overtake all of us. When we are young we like to think it is a long way off and perhaps do not dwell on it very much. But before our own deaths most of us will have to face the death of someone close to us. So it is not something which can simply be put out of our minds. It is interesting to see that all religions have a lot to say about death. They all teach that the end of this life on earth is not the final end of a person. They believe that life goes on somehow and that during this present life we should be preparing ourselves for the next. The Koran says:

Say: 'The death from which you shrink is sure to overtake you. Then you shall be sent back to Him who knows the visible and the unseen, and He will declare to you all that you have done. (*Chapter 62 verse 8*)

In Islam, life after death is seen as a continuation and direct result of our lives now. It teaches that those who are close to God in this earthly life and obey his commands, will be with him in heaven; whereas those who turn their backs on God and live wicked lives will go to hell. This subject is found throughout the Koran, particularly in the earliest chapters that Muhammad recited, which are the shortest and found at the end of the book. Here people are warned of the dreadful last day of judgement to come when each

Fig.12. Muslims believe in life after death. The dead are buried lying on their sides with their heads pointing towards Mecca, to await resurrection on the day of judgement when they will be sent to heaven or hell. The cemeteries, like this one in Morocco, should just have raised mounds over the bodies and simple headstones.

person will be called to account for everything he or she has done. The titles of some of these chapters refer to this last day: 'The Earthquake' which begins 'When Earth is rocked in her last convulsion...', and 'The Cessation', 'The Disaster', 'The Overwhelming Event' and others. The chapter called 'The Cataclysm' has these words:

> When the sky is rent asunder; when the stars scatter and the oceans roll together; when the graves are hurled about; each soul shall know what it has done and what it has failed to do. (*Chapter 82 verse 1*)

On the other hand there are chapters with headings like 'The Merciful'. In fact, in most chapters both sides of the picture are described. For instance the chapter called 'The Resurrection' says this:

> On that day there shall be joyous faces, looking towards their Lord. On that day there shall be mournful faces, dreading some great affliction. (*Chapter 75 verse 20*)

Life after death is described in the Koran in a physical way and many Muslims accept it as such, rather than in a spiritual sense. It is for this reason that Muslims do not practise cremation. They do not burn up their dead bodies but bury them quickly before they begin to decay. For they believe that everyone will be raised to life again on the day of judgement. The Koran says:

> Does man think We shall never put his bones together again? Indeed, We can remould his very fingers. (*Chapter 75 verse 2*)

Heaven and hell are described as actual places, as in these passages:

> But when the supreme day arrives. . . those that transgressed and chose their present life will find themselves in Hell; but those that feared to stand before their Lord and curbed their souls' desires shall dwell in Paradise. (*Chapter 79 verses 35 – 41*)

> On that day there shall be downcast faces, of men broken and worn out, burnt by a scorching fire, drinking from a seething fountain. Their only food shall be bitter thorns, which will neither sustain them nor satisfy their hunger.
> On that day there shall be radiant faces, of men well-pleased with their labours, in a lofty garden. There they shall hear no idle talk. A gushing fountain shall be there, and raised soft couches with goblets placed before them; silken cushions ranged in order and carpets richly spread. (*Chapter 88 verses 2 – 18*)

So it is believed that everyone is given his just reward in the hereafter. If he believes in God and asks him to forgive his wrongdoings, then God will be merciful. But the Koran teaches that those who reject God will live to regret it.

When a person dies in Islam it is therefore not regarded as the end of him or her, even though the bereaved family and friends are still naturally sad. They regard this death, like everything else which happens, as being in accordance with God's will. They believe that one day that person will be brought back to life and, if God wishes it, will be reunited with them in paradise.

On first hearing that someone has died, a Muslim quotes these words from the Koran:

> We belong to Allah, and to Him we shall return. (*Chapter 2 verse 156*)

Then relatives and friends gather at the dead person's house to comfort each other, recite the Koran and pray for God's mercy on the person who has died. The body is prepared for burial by members of the same sex. It is washed, wrapped in one or two clean white sheets, and laid on a stretcher or in a coffin. Then the men carry the body on their shoulders either to the mosque or straight to the burial ground for the funeral prayers. These are said together by at least some of them before the body is lowered into the ground and buried with its face towards Mecca. The period of mourning can last just a few days or sometimes as long as forty days. During this time all those related to the dead person, even distant relatives, behave in a sombre manner and are not allowed to attend any joyful events like parties and weddings. After this time they will continue to visit the grave of their loved one and this will make them think seriously about the whole issue of death.

Make sure you know
1 how Muslims deal with their dead bodies
2 what they think will happen on the last day

See if you understand
3 why Muslims do not practise cremation
4 why, according to their belief, some people will go to heaven and others to hell

Issues to discuss
5 Why do Muslims believe so strongly in life after death? Can you think of any other reasons for believing in some sort of existence beyond this earthly life?
6 Muslims are very careful how they live this life because they think they will be rewarded or punished for it in the hereafter. If there were no life after death, would it still matter how we live now?

13 Subdivisions within Islam

Despite the emphasis on unity and brotherhood within Islam, there are subdivisions within it. Generally they are fairly tolerant of one another; mosques are open to all Muslims and intermarriage between all Muslims is usually permitted.

The most important division is between the Sunni and Shi'a Muslims, there being about one of the latter to every five of the former. There are many points of contact between the Sunni and the Shi'a: both accept the Koran and the Hadith as their main guides to Islam, and they follow the same basic 'pillars'. It has been said that the Shi'ites have been influenced to a greater extent by outside beliefs. They have introduced elements into Islam which seem to satisfy a deep religious need for many people, such as the need for saints and pilgrimages, and a greater intensity of personal devotion, in contrast to the more formal worship of the Sunni.

It is not certain when these two parties first separated from each other, but their quarrel relates to Muhammad's successor. On Muhammad's death one of his earliest followers, or Companions, named Abu Bakr, took over the leadership of the Islamic state and was known as the caliph, or 'Successor' to Muhammad. The caliphate passed from one caliph to another at their deaths, until it came eventually to 'Ali, the fourth caliph. 'Ali was Muhammad's cousin and son-in-law, being married to Muhammad's daughter, Fatima. As a leader he proved to be rather weak, and was unable to cope with a rival claimant to his power, named Mu'awiya. 'Ali was eventually assassinated and his son Hasan resigned the caliphate to Mu'awiya. Hasan died a few years later and 'Ali's second son Husayn tried to reclaim the caliphate by force but was killed in battle.

The Shi'ites claim that 'Ali was Muhammad's true heir and successor, and their name means 'party' of 'Ali. They believe that God guided Muhammad to appoint 'Ali and that the first three caliphs were therefore usurpers. Some Shi'ites even curse them in their Friday prayers, and all Shi'ites add to their statement of belief: 'and 'Ali is the friend of God'. They believe that 'Ali's sons should have succeeded him and therefore refuse to recognise the official, Sunni line of caliphs, having their own line of Imams who

Fig.13. This photograph was taken at the Shi'i celebration of 10th. Muharram in Hyderabad, Pakistan. During the procession Muslims beat their chests and backs with chains to share in the suffering of Husayn whose martyrdom they are remembering.

each designated his successor. Because of this refusal to recognise the official government, the Shi'ites gained the support of many other discontented people within the Islamic empire and were often rebellious minority groups, developing their own secret teachings. Because they attracted people who had been forcibly converted to Islam from other religions, and who therefore bore a grudge against the official religion, the Shi'ites were more easily influenced by ideas from these other religions.

'Ali, Hasan and Husayn became the great martyrs of the Shi'ites, (they claim that Mu'awiya poisoned Hasan), and each year the martyrdom of Husayn is remembered in a ten-day period of mourning. During this time the men dress in black and the women in black or green. They meet for sermons on Islam and on the saintliness of Husayn and his family, and models of Husayn's tomb at Karbala are used to focus their attention on his death. The final day of mourning is the 10th. Muharram, the day of Husayn's death. On this day the women break their glass bangles (usually done when a woman's husband dies), and models of the tomb are carried in a great procession. Many of the followers beat their breasts and the men often whip themselves until they draw blood, in an effort to share in Husayn's suffering (see Fig.13). In Kazimayn, just outside Baghdad in Iraq, a passion play is acted out on this tenth day. Forty days later another play is performed at Husayn's shrine in Karbala, called 'The Return of the Head'. This reminds the Shi'ites that when Husayn was killed his head was cut off and taken in triumph to the capital city of Damascus in Syria; but it was returned 40 days later and buried with his body in Karbala. This annual celebration of Husayn's death, in which all Shi'ites join so fervently, has taught them to be prepared to sacrifice themselves in this life for the sake of a spiritual reward.

The Shi'ites are broken down into further groups, the main two being the Twelvers (or Imamis) and the Seveners (or Ismailis). Most Shi'ites belong to the Twelvers, whose main home is in Iran. Their name comes from the fact that they had twelve imams (the word means a 'divinely chosen' or 'divinely inspired' leader). They claim that the twelfth, Muhammad al-Muntazar, did not die but disappeared in 880 C.E., and they believe this 'hidden imam' will return as the Mahdi, or 'divinely guided' one, to deliver them at the end of the world. The Twelvers regard all twelve imams as revelations of God and say special prayers for them.

The Seveners accept only seven imams. They disagree with the Twelvers and claim that Ismail was the rightful seventh imam. The Seveners believe that Ismail is the 'hidden imam' who will return as the Mahdi, and that he was actually God in human form. They developed into minor, secretive movements, which tended to attract the more rebellious and extremist elements in the population. One famous Sevener group of the twelfth and thirteenth centuries C.E. was known as the Assassins (or Hashishi). They were a terrorist group who held out in the mountains of Persia and committed violent and daring crimes against the government under the influence of hashish. The Aga Khan, the spiritual head of the majority of Seveners today, is said to be a direct descendant of Hasan Sabbah, the founder of this movement. The Aga Khan has a following of over ten million Seveners, scattered throughout Africa and Asia. Recently there have been attempts to bring them more in line with the rest of Islam but they still have many different beliefs and worship in 'gathering houses' (called jama'at khanah) rather than mosques.

We have seen that the Shi'ites venerate 'Ali; in order to discover yet another sect within Islam, let us return to his death. He was assassinated by an extremist group known as the Kharijites. They expected every Muslim to be totally committed to his religion and emphasised the need for purity in thought, word and deed. They were very influential in the early history of Islam and still have some followers today in small, scattered communities in Algeria, Tunisia, Tanzania and Oman.

Something of the spirit and influence of the Kharijites lives on in the modern Wahhabi movement in Saudi Arabia. This began in the eighteenth century C.E. and is named after its founder 'Abd-al-Wahhab. The Wahhabis prefer to call themselves simply 'Muslims' since they regard themselves as the true Muslims who have tried to return to the Islam of Muhammad's day. Another name they use for themselves is the Unitarians because they emphasise the oneness, or unity, of God and therefore reject all devotion to angels, saints or prophets since some people have prayed to them instead of God. For the same reason they have tried to prevent the veneration which goes on at the tombs of holy people and they even removed the markers from the graves of Muhammad's family and the Companions in Medina. They believe Islam has become corrupted by ideas and practices from outside and has become religiously and morally lax. They are therefore extremely puritanical in their worship and everyday lives. Their mosques are very plain and they try to say all their prayers there rather than in the home. They dress very simply, wear no gold jewelry, have no music, do not smoke, do not use bad language and are never frivolous. This movement has been supported by the Saudi Dynasty which has encouraged a strict form of Islam even in the face of increased national wealth and contact with the West.

Make sure you know
1 the names of the two main Shi'i sects
2 the name of the person who was regarded by the Shi'ites as the rightful successor to Muhammad

See if you understand
3 why the Shi'ites celebrate Husayn's death
4 why there are many beliefs and practices in Shi'a Islam which are not found among the Sunnis

Issues to discuss
5 Islam has split into several main divisions and many minor ones. Do you think this is understandable in the development of a major world religion like Islam? What factors would influence this process?
6 Do you think the Wahhabi Muslims are right to try to keep strictly to the type of Islam that existed in Muhammad's time? Does it matter that a religion develops new ideas and practices as time goes by?

14 Holy War

From its very beginning Islam was a force to be reckoned with. The speed at which it grew is truly amazing. By the time of Muhammad's death most of Arabia had already been won over to Islam, and it very quickly spread beyond there. Spurred on by a single-minded devotion to Allah, and the thought of a reward in heaven for soldiers who were killed in battle, the Muslim armies swept out of the desert, bringing the surrounding empires to their knees.

Within a century Islam had spread westwards through Egypt and North Africa into Spain, even entering France at one stage; and eastwards through Palestine, Syria and Persia, deep into central Asia. Wherever the Arabs went, people were encouraged to accept Islam as their religion, although Jews and Christians were tolerated as long as they remained law-abiding citizens. Through a large part of the world they spread the Muslim way of life, their art and architecture, their alphabet, language and literature, and their learning. The world owes the Arabs much, particularly in the spheres of chemistry, astronomy, mathematics and medicine.

Some people think it strange that a religion was spread by force of arms, but there has always been within Islam the idea of Holy War, known as jihad. There have even been attempts to regard this as the sixth pillar of Islam. This is the idea that sometimes it is right to fight for God: to use physical force to defend what is right and to bring about something which is good. In one passage the Koran says:

> Fight for the sake of Allah those that fight against you, but do not attack them first. Allah does not love the aggressors. Fight against them until idolatry is no more and Allah's religion reigns supreme. But if they mend their ways, fight none except the evil-doers. (*Chapter 2 verses 190 – 193*)

Muslims are proud of their history of conquest for they regard the success of the Arab armies as proof that God was on their side. They believe that the world would be a better place if all men became Muslims, united in their worship of the one, true God and obeying his commands. However, as time went on, Holy War

Fig.14. In Istanbul, Turkey, stands the Sultan Ahmet Mosque, built 1609–1616 C.E. and known to foreigners as the Blue Mosque because of the blue ceramic tiling inside. It is famous for its six minarets. Istanbul was the centre of the Ottoman Empire.

became hedged about with all sorts of safeguards. It was said that a war was only holy if it was in self-defence, had the approval of an imam, was likely to be successful and had the support of the soldiers themselves so that they were determined to win.

Today many Muslims regard Holy War as more of a spiritual thing. There are fewer opportunities for them actually to take up arms for their beliefs, but they *can* fight the impulses to do wrong which everyone finds within his own self. Indeed, Muhammad himself called this inner struggle the Greater Holy War. 'Jihad' literally means 'striving' and Islam argues that you should not just sit back and bemoan things which are wrong in the world, but actively set out to change them. Islam believes that each individual should be prepared to give up everything, even his own life, for the cause of right.

For well over a thousand years Islam was a great world power. The leaders of the Islamic empire were known as caliphs and this caliphate continued right into the twentieth century C.E. At first the caliphs were truly religious men, being the original Companions of Muhammad, but it was not long before this leadership became hereditary so that a son inherited the throne from his father. The first family to rule in this way was the Ummayad Dynasty which ruled, not from Medina, but from Damascus in Syria. The next, the Abbasid Dynasty, which came to power in 750 C.E., ruled from Baghdad in Persia (now in Iraq).

The Abbasids were finally overthrown by fierce warriors from China known as the Moghuls or Mongols. The famous Jenghiz Kahn captured Baghdad in 1258 C.E. Yet these savage conquerors became tamed by Islam and for a time the Moghul empire led the Muslim world. It ruled the subcontinent of India until the British took over there.

Finally, the Ottoman empire of Turkey was the last and the greatest Islamic dynasty. It was at the height of its power 450 years ago, ruling the Muslim empire from Istanbul (see Fig.14). It survived longer than any other of the dynasties, finally coming to an end in 1924, after the First World War.

Make sure you know
1 the meaning of Holy War, apart from taking up arms
2 the name of the last and longest surviving Muslim empire

See if you understand
3 why Jews and Christians were allowed to continue their own religions
4 why the world is indebted to the Muslims

Issues to discuss
5 Do you think the Muslims are right in saying that violence is sometimes necessary? How would a pacifist answer them?
6 Do you agree with Islam in arguing that the end justifies the means? Is this morally right?

15 Muslim countries today

Up until about 200 years ago the history of Islam was largely a success story. Then the Islamic Empire gradually broke down and many Muslim countries came under non-Muslim rule. This was unfortunate for the Muslim populations because it meant that the laws of the land were no longer the Islamic laws, known as the Sharia, in which Islam sees no division between religion and politics. Muhammad had been both prophet and judge and had set up an Islamic state where people tried to live in accordance with God's will. In Islamic countries it is the religious scholars, called the 'Ulama, who work out the laws.

One example of a Muslim minority population is in Israel which was set up as a Jewish state in 1948. This country was originally called Palestine and inhabited largely by Muslim Arabs. Then the Jews began to arrive in great numbers after the Second World War and many Muslims fled as refugees to the Gaza Strip and the surrounding Muslim countries of Jordan, Syria and Lebanon, so that there are now only half a million left in Israel. The capital city of Jerusalem, which is holy for Jews, Muslims and Christians, was at first divided between the Jewish and Muslim people there, but in 1967 this too was won over by the Jews. The law of the land takes priority over the religious courts. For instance, polygamy is illegal, although the Koran permits it; there is a minimum age of seventeen for marriage, although Muslims traditionally marry young; and divorce is only allowed if *both* husband and wife agree. At first the neighbouring country of Egypt supported the Palestinians in their struggle against Israel, but after suffering defeats in several wars, Egypt eventually negotiated for permanent peace. Early in 1980 the main road between Egypt and Israel was opened for the first time in over 30 years.

In other places, the second half of this century has seen a reassertion of Islam, so that many Muslim countries protested against Egypt's policy of reconciliation. This revival of Islam has been due to individual Muslim countries gaining their independence and enforcing Islamic laws once more, rather than the re-establishment of a united Islamic state which cuts across national boundaries. It is true that there have been various attempts at co-

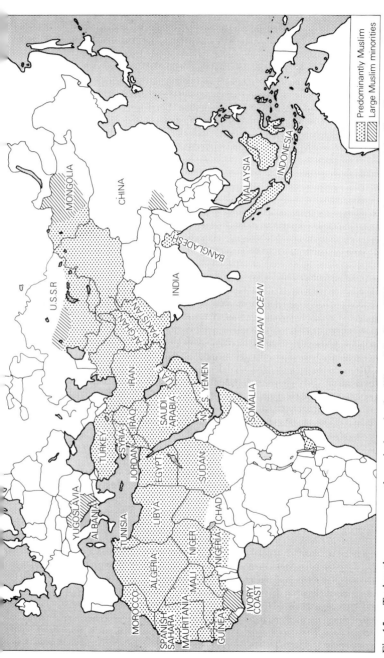

Fig. 15.　Today there are more than six hundred million Muslims. This map shows where most Muslims live.

Predominantly Muslim

Large Muslim minorities

59

operation between different Muslim countries, but there is no country strong enough to unite them all, and Islam has developed separately within each of them.

Of all the Muslim countries to reassert themselves, only Turkey tried to turn its back on its Muslim past in order to compete with the modern Western world. A civil war in 1920 C.E. threw up 'Ataturk' as the leader of the new Turkish Republic. He became known as the 'Father of Modern Turkey' because of his reforms. The Arabic alphabet was abandoned and the Western calendar adopted, people were forced to choose European type surnames and Ankara became the new, modern capital instead of the ancient city of Istanbul. New laws were adopted, women were given equal rights to men, and the old religious courts were closed. Religious practices were discouraged, many famous mosques were turned into museums, and religious education was stopped. But Islam proved to be too deeply embedded in the lives of the people and when free elections were allowed in 1950 C.E. the vast majority showed that they wanted their old, Muslim way of life to be restored. So changes are now going ahead far more slowly and there is a more tolerant attitude towards religion.

At the other extreme is Saudi Arabia, the country which is guardian of the holy cities of Mecca and Medina. It owns the largest known oil reserves of any country in the world and over the last 40 years has been able to develop its industry, technology and communications with the outside world. Yet despite its new-found wealth and rapid modernisation it has tried to maintain a very strict form of Islam as the basis of its society. It enforces the Islamic laws so that, for instance, no alcohol or pig meat is allowed to be imported, since these are forbidden to Muslims. Its criminal law is regarded as very harsh by outsiders, imposing the Koranic punishment of cutting off the hands of persistent thieves. All punishments are carried out in public to deter others and show them that justice is being done. Men and women are kept apart in public, with segregated schools and colleges, and women are not allowed to drive cars. So it is clear that Saudi Arabia is determined to resist the spread of Western values and, with its wealth, it has considerable influence in the Islamic world.

Other Muslim countries fall between the two extremes of Turkey and Saudi Arabia. For instance, Pakistan was formed in 1947 when it was separated from India and set itself up as the 'Pure Homeland' for Muslims and eventually established a capital city called Islamabad, or 'The City of Islam'. (Its eastern territory has since broken away as Bangladesh). Up until 1977 C.E. when General Zia ul-Haq took control, the leaders of Pakistan had not gone far in putting the ideals of Islam into practice; but with 98 per cent of the population being Muslims there was wide support for

60

General Zia's enforcement of a stricter Islamic system.

In Iran, popular support for an Islamic state has also won the day. Iran is the chief home of the Shi'i Muslims. This branch of Islam started by rejecting the official government of its day and has often been involved in political uprisings since then. In 1978 C.E. there was a popular rebellion in Iran against the ruler who was known as the Shah. This was spurred on by the religious leaders, the highest rank being that of 'ayatollah' which means 'sign of God'. For the rebel population it was a holy war and many pledged themselves to fight to the death in the cause of Islam. They rallied under the leadership of the Ayatollah Khomeini who had returned from exile and early in 1979 the Shah was forced to flee for his life. The country became ruled by religious leaders who were determined to bring back strict Islamic laws and to resist Western influences.

There are of course many other Muslim countries (see Fig.15), all enforcing Islamic laws to differing degrees and interpreting Islamic ideals in different ways. An interesting expansion of Islam is to be seen in the continent of Africa where this religion is winning many new converts; and also amongst the black population of the United States. In the Soviet Union too, the number of Muslims is increasing, mainly because of their high birth rate. Some estimates even suggest that they could number up to one third of the population there by the turn of the century. In Indonesia already 90 per cent of the population are Muslims. They have incorporated Islam with their earlier culture so that there is now a great variety of beliefs and practices.

So Islam will certainly continue to make an impact on the world.

Make sure you know
1 the names of at least two Muslim countries in North Africa
2 which Muslim country deliberately tried to become westernised
3 in which country Mecca and Medina are found
4 the name of a Muslim country where there has been a lot of political unrest

See if you understand
5 why Pakistan broke away from India
6 why some Muslim countries segregate men and women in public

Issues to discuss
7 What do you think about people being punished in public, as happens in some Muslim countries? Do you think you would attend a public hanging?
8 What is there about Western society which Muslims might regard as corrupt?

List of Arabic words

In the study of Islam you will come across a lot of Arabic words. Sometimes you will find them spelt in different ways because Arabic letters are different from ours and scholars disagree over how they should be put into our Latin alphabet. Here is a list of all the Arabic words used in this book, with their meanings.

Adhan	'announcement'—call to prayer
Allah	'The God'—name for God
ayatollah	'sign of God'—religious leader in Shi'a Islam
caliph	'successor' to Muhammad—ruler of the Islamic empire
Dhul-Hijja	twelfth month—month of the Major Pilgrimage
eid	'festival'
Eid-ul-Adha	'Great Festival'—the Festival of Sacrifice after the Major Pilgrimage
Eid-ul-Fitr	'Little Festival'—the Festival of Fast Breaking after Ramadan
Hadith	'statement'—the carefully verified collections of stories of what Muhammad said and did
Hajj	the Major Pilgrimage—fifth pillar of Islam
Hajji	a pilgrim—someone who has completed the Hajj
halal	'permitted' e.g. halal meat has been ritually slaughtered in the name of God, and has the blood drained from it.
Hanif	'one who is inclined', i.e. to believe in one God
Hijra	'Emigration'—when Muhammad left Mecca for Medina
imam	'he who stands at the front'—prayer leader
Islam	'surrender' (noun)—the name of the religion
Islamic	of Islam (adjective)
jama'at khanah	'gathering house'—place of worship for Shi'i Seveners
jihad	'striving'—holy war or a struggle of the spirit
Kaaba	'cube'—the central shrine, in Mecca

Koran	'recitation'—name of the holy book (also spelt Qur'an)
Labbaika	'Doubly at your service O God'—cry of the pilgrims
Mahdi	'divinely guided'—leader expected by Shi'ites to come at the end of the world
Mecca	city in Arabia which is the centre of Islam (also spelt Makka)
Medina-al-Nabi	'City of the Prophet'—known as Medina
mihrab	alcove in wall of mosque showing the direction of Mecca
minaret	tall tower usually built onto mosques
mosque	place of 'prostration'—building in which Muslims gather for prayer and education
muezzin	man who calls Muslims to prayer
Muhammad	name of the Holy Prophet (also spelt Mohammed)
Muharram	first month in the Muslim year
Muslim	one who 'surrenders' himself to God—a follower of Islam; (adjective) of the culture of Islam
Qadr	power and glory—refers to the Night of Power when Muhammad first began to receive the Koran
Rabi'ul-Awwal	third month—sacred because of Muhammad's birthday
rakah	the complete sequence of movements for prayer
Ramadan	ninth month—month of fasting, fourth pillar of Islam
salat	prayer i.e. five daily prayers, second pillar of Islam (pronounced salah)
salm	'peace'—possibly connected with the word 'Islam'
sawm	a fast
Shahada	the statement of faith
Sharia	'highway'—Islamic law
Shi'a	'party'—name of an important branch of Islam—the party of 'Ali
Shi'i	(adjective) of Shi'a Islam
Shi'ite	a member of Shi'a Islam
subha	a string of prayer beads
Sunni	comes from 'sunnah' meaning 'path' i.e. one who follows the right path—name of the main branch of Islam
sura	chapter of the Koran—there are 114 in all
'Ulama	'the learned'—religious scholars who interpret Islamic law
Yaum ul-Juma't	'Day of Assembly'—Friday
Zakat	'purification'—name of the tax Muslims must pay to charity, third pillar of Islam

Useful Addresses
The Islamic Cultural Centre,
146 Park Road, London NW8 7RG.

Minaret House,
9 Leslie Park Road,
East Croydon, Surrey CRO 6TN.

Muslim Educational Trust,
130 Stroud Green Road,
London N4 3RZ.

Islamic Council of Europe,
16 Grosvenor Crescent,
London SW1 7EP.

The Islamic Foundation,
223 London Road,
Leicester LE2 12E.

Islamic Book Centre
120 Drummond Street
London NW1 2HL

Index